Rain, Rain, Rain!

Written by
Rob Waring and **Maurice Jamall**

to fall off a bike

to get dressed

to get on a bike

to ride

to run

bus

clock

dog

gate

holiday

rain

train

cold

late

wet

In the story

Faye

Faye's mother

"Oh, no! It's Monday today. And I have school,"
thinks Faye.
She is looking at the rain. "I don't like the rain.
And it's raining today."
She thinks, "I don't want to go to school."

School starts at 9 o'clock. Now it's 8:20!
She looks at the clock.
"Oh no," she thinks. "I'm late for school!"
Faye gets dressed.

"Good morning, Faye," says her mother.

"Morning, Mom," she says.

Her mother says, "Please eat, Faye."

"Sorry, Mom, I'm late," says Faye.

"Late? Where are you going?" asks her mother.

"School," she says.

"But Faye . . . ," says her mother.
"Sorry, mom, I'm late. See you!" says Faye.
Faye's mother says, "But . . . , but . . ."
"Bye!" says Faye.
Faye runs out of the house.

Faye gets on her bike. Every day, Faye takes the train to school.

She rides to the train station on her bike.

She looks at her watch. She thinks, "I'm late. Oh, no! It's 8:35."

"And it's raining. I don't like the rain," she thinks.

The rain is coming down. Faye is getting wet.
A girl is walking a dog. Faye does not see the girl
and the dog.
"Look out," says the girl. Faye's bike hits the dog.
"I'm sorry," Faye says.
Faye falls off her bike. "Oh, no! My bike!" she says.

Faye gets up. "I'm very late,"
she thinks.

Faye pushes her bike to the station.
She is cold and very wet.

She sees the station. She goes to the
bike rack.

Faye puts her bike in the bike rack.
She looks at the clock. It's now 8:45.
"Good," she thinks. "The station is there."
Faye goes into the station.

"But where's the train?" she thinks.
A man says, "There are no trains today."
She sees a tree in front of the train.
"Oh no!" thinks Faye. "No trains today!"
She looks at her watch. It's now 8:47.

"What do I do?" she thinks. "School starts at 9 o'clock!"
Faye thinks, "How do I get to the school?"
She thinks, "Oh, the bus! The bus goes to the school!"
She runs to the bus station, but the bus is leaving.
"Wait for me!" she says. But the bus does not wait.

Faye waits for the next bus. She waits and waits.
There is no bus. "Where's the bus?" thinks Faye.
Faye does not see a car.
The car goes into the water. Now she is very very wet.

"Oh no! It is now 8:49," she thinks.
She runs to school. She's very cold and very wet.
A boy and girl are looking at Faye.
"Why is she running?" they think.

Faye runs and runs. She sees the school gate.
She thinks, "Good! There's the school."
She looks at her watch. It is 8:59.
"Good, I'm not late," she thinks.

Faye gets to school. She sees something on the school gate.
It says, "*No school today. School holiday.*"
"Oh no!" she thinks. "There's no school today."
"It's a school holiday. Oh no!" she says.